Made in the USA
Columbia, SC
13 June 2023

18026424R00067